Mastering Your Money: A Comprehensive Guide to Financial Literacy

Chapter 1: Master your Money

Step 1: Understanding Your Financial Situation

- Start by taking an inventory of your financial situation:

+ Make a list of all your income sources (wages, investments, etc.)

+ Make a list of all your expenses (housing, food, transportation, etc.)

+ Make a list of your debts (credit cards, loans, etc.)

+ Make a list of your assets (savings, investments, etc.)

1. Calculate your net worth by subtracting your total expenses from your total income.
2. Identify areas where you can cut back on unnecessary expenses and allocate that money towards debt repayment or savings.

Step 2: Setting Financial Goals

- Set specific, measurable, achievable, relevant, and time-bound (SMART) financial goals:

+ Short-term goals (less than 1 year): pay off debt, build an emergency fund, etc.

+ Medium-term goals (1-5 years): save for a down payment on a house, retire high-interest debt, etc.

+ Long-term goals (5+ years): save for retirement, achieve financial independence, etc.

1. Prioritize your goals based on importance and urgency.

Step 3: Budgeting and Expense Management

- Create a budget that accounts for 50-30-20:

+ 50% of income towards necessary expenses (housing, utilities, food, etc.)

+ 30% towards discretionary spending (entertainment, hobbies, etc.)

+ 20% towards saving and debt repayment

- Track your expenses to stay within budget:

+ Use a budgeting app or spreadsheet to track your spending

+ Categorize expenses into needs vs. wants

+ Adjust budget as needed to stay on track

Step 4: Managing Debt

- Prioritize debt repayment by focusing on high-interest debt first:

+ Create a debt snowball by paying off smallest balances first

+ Consider consolidating debt into a single loan with a lower interest rate

- Pay more than the minimum payment to pay off debt faster:

+ Consider using the avalanche method (paying off debt with the highest interest rate first)

+ Consider using the snowball method (paying off debt with the smallest balance first)

Step 5: Building an Emergency Fund

- Aim to save 3-6 months' worth of living expenses in an easily accessible savings account:

+ Use this fund to cover unexpected expenses and avoid going into debt.

+ Consider setting aside extra funds for specific expenses like car repairs or medical bills.

Step 6: Investing and Growing Your Wealth

- Start investing early to take advantage of compound interest:

+ Consider contributing to a 401(k) or IRA for retirement savings

+ Consider opening a brokerage account to invest in stocks or other investments

- Diversify your investments to minimize risk:

+ Spread investments across different asset classes (stocks, bonds, real estate, etc.)

+ Consider working with a financial advisor to create a customized investment plan

Step 7: Protecting Your Financial Future

- Consider purchasing insurance to protect against unexpected events:

+ Life insurance to provide for loved ones in case of death

+ Disability insurance to provide income if unable to work

+ Health insurance to cover medical expenses

- Plan for long-term care and potential retirement costs:

+ Research long-term care options and costs

+ Consider purchasing long-term care insurance

Step 8: Educating Yourself and Staying Disciplined

- Continuously educate yourself on personal finance topics:

+ Read books and articles on personal finance

+ Take online courses or attend seminars on personal finance

- Stay disciplined and avoid lifestyle inflation:

+ Avoid overspending and sticking to your budget

+ Avoid getting caught up in keeping up with the Joneses

- Additional Tips and Reminders:
1. Avoid impulse purchases and prioritize needs over wants
2. Take advantage of employer-matched retirement accounts like 401(k) or 403(b)
3. Consider automating savings and bill payments to reduce errors and overspending
4. Review and adjust your budget regularly to stay on track
5. Avoid making excuses or procrastinating – take action towards achieving your financial goals!

- Common Mistakes to Avoid:
1. Not having an emergency fund or not prioritizing savings
2. Not paying off high-interest debt or consolidating debt into a single loan with a higher interest rate
3. Not investing for retirement or not diversifying investments
4. Not educating yourself on personal finance topics or not staying disciplined

By following these steps and avoiding common mistakes, you can master your money and achieve financial literacy. Remember to stay patient, stay disciplined, and prioritize your financial goals.

Chapter 2: *Creating a Budge*

Step 1: Identify Your Income

- Start by calculating your total monthly income from all sources, including:

+ Salary or wages

+ Investments

+ Freelance work

+ Any other regular income

- Write down the amount of your total monthly income

Step 2: Categorize Your Expenses

- Divide your expenses into categories, such as:

+ Housing (rent/mortgage, utilities, insurance)

+ Transportation (car payment, gas, insurance, maintenance)

+ Food and groceries

+ Entertainment (dining out, movies, hobbies)

+ Debt repayment (credit cards, loans)

+ Savings

+ Insurance (health, life, disability)

+ Miscellaneous (gifts, subscriptions, unexpected expenses)

Step 3: Set Financial Goals

- Determine what you want to achieve with your budget. Do you want to:

+ Save for a specific goal, such as a down payment on a house or a vacation?

+ Pay off debt?

+ Increase your savings rate?

- Write down your financial goals and prioritize them.

Step 4: Assign Percentages

- Allocate a percentage of your income to each category based on your goals and priorities. A general rule of thumb is:

+ Housing: 30%

+ Transportation: 10-15%

+ Food and groceries: 10-15%

+ Entertainment: 5-10%

+ Debt repayment: 5-10%

+ Savings: 10-20%

+ Insurance: 5%

+ Miscellaneous: 5%

Step 5: Assign Dollar Amounts

- Take the percentages from Step 4 and multiply them by your total monthly income from Step 1 to get a dollar amount for each category.
- For example, if your total monthly income is $4,000 and you allocated 30% to housing, you would allocate $1,200 per month to housing.

Step 6: Track Your Expenses

1. Keep track of every single transaction you make for a month to see where your money is going.
2. Use a budgeting app, spreadsheet, or simply write it down in a notebook.
3. This will help you identify areas where you can cut back and make adjustments to your budget.

Step 7: Adjust and Refine

- Review your budget regularly (e.g. every few months) to see if you need to make any adjustments.
- Ask yourself:

+ Is this expense necessary?

+ Can I cut back on this expense?

+ Am I meeting my financial goals?

- Make adjustments as needed to stay on track.

Notes:

1. Be realistic when creating your budget. Don't try to make drastic changes all at once.
2. Prioritize needs over wants. Make sure you're covering essential expenses like housing and food before allocating money to discretionary spending.
3. Consider using the 50/30/20 rule: 50% of your income goes towards necessary expenses, 30% towards discretionary spending, and 20% towards savings and debt repayment.
4. Don't forget to budget for irregular expenses like car maintenance or property taxes.
5. Consider automating your savings by setting up automatic transfers from your checking account to your savings or investment accounts.
6. Review your budget with a financial advisor or trusted friend/family member to get an outside perspective.

Additional Tips:

1. Use cash instead of credit cards for discretionary spending to help stick to your budget.
2. Take advantage of employer-matched retirement accounts like 401(k) or IRA.
3. Consider using the envelope system: divide your expenses into categories and place the corresponding amount of cash into an envelope for each category.
4. Don't forget to budget for self-care and personal development expenses like gym memberships or online courses.

By following these steps and notes, you'll be well on your way to creating a budget that helps you achieve your financial goals. Remember to regularly review and adjust your budget to stay on track!

Chapter 3: Building an Emergency Fund

An emergency fund is a stash of money set aside for unexpected expenses, such as car repairs or medical bills. This chapter will explain why an emergency fund is essential and provide tips on how to build one.

★ Why Do I Need an Emergency Fund?

An emergency fund is a crucial component of personal finance that helps you navigate unexpected expenses, financial shocks, and unexpected events. Without one, you may struggle to cover essential expenses, accumulate debt, and put your financial future at risk. Here's why you need an emergency fund:

- ✓ Unemployment: Job loss or reduction in income can be a significant financial shock.
- ✓ Medical emergencies: Illnesses, accidents, or surgeries can lead to unexpected medical bills.
- ✓ Car repairs: Breakdowns, accidents, or maintenance issues can be costly.
- ✓ Home repairs: Roof leaks, plumbing issues, or other unexpected expenses can arise.

- ✓ Natural disasters: Weather-related events like hurricanes, floods, or wildfires can cause destruction and damage.

- ★ How Much Should I Save?

The general rule of thumb is to save 3-6 months' worth of living expenses in an easily accessible savings account. This amount will help you cover essential expenses during a financial crisis. However, the right amount for you will depend on factors such as:

- ✗ Your income stability
- ✗ Job security
- ✗ Debt obligations
- ✗ Family size and dependents
- ✗ Geographic location (e.g., areas prone to natural disasters)

Step-by-Step Guide to Building an Emergency Fund

Step 1: Assess Your Finances

- Start by tracking your income and expenses for a month to understand where your money is going. You can use a budgeting app or spreadsheet to make it easier.

Step 2: Calculate Your Essential Expenses

- Identify essential expenses that you would need to cover during an emergency, such as:

* Rent/mortgage

* Utilities (electricity, water, gas)

* Food

* Transportation (car payment, insurance, gas)

* Minimum debt payments (credit cards, loans)

* Insurance premiums (health, life, disability)

Step 3: Determine Your Monthly Essential Expenses

- Add up the total amount of your essential expenses to determine your monthly essential expense amount.

Step 4: Calculate Your Emergency Fund Goal

- Multiply your monthly essential expense amount by the number of months you want to cover in your emergency fund (3-6 months).

Example: If your monthly essential expenses are $3,500 and you want to cover 4 months of expenses, your emergency fund goal would be $14,000 (3,500 x 4).

Step 5: Start Building Your Emergency Fund

- Open a dedicated savings account specifically for your emergency fund. You can choose a high-yield savings account or a money market account that offers easy access to your funds.

Step 6: Automate Your Savings

- Set up automatic transfers from your primary checking account to your emergency fund account. You can set up bi-weekly or monthly transfers to reach your goal faster.

Step 7: Adjust Your Budget

- Reduce discretionary spending to free up more money for your emergency fund. Consider ways to cut costs on non-essential expenses like dining out, entertainment, and hobbies.

Step 8: Monitor and Adjust

- Regularly review your progress toward your emergency fund goal. Adjust your transfer amounts or budget as needed to stay on track.

Additional Tips and Considerations

1. Consider keeping some cash on hand for immediate needs.
2. Review and update your emergency fund regularly as your income and expenses change.
3. Avoid dipping into retirement accounts or other long-term savings for emergency funds.
4. Consider using tax-advantaged accounts like Health Savings Accounts (HSAs) for medical emergencies.
5. Make sure you have the right insurance coverage (health, disability, etc.) to minimize financial risk.

Building an emergency fund is a crucial step towards achieving financial stability and peace of mind. By following these steps and committing to regular savings habits, you'll be better prepared to handle unexpected events and keep your finances on track. Remember to regularly review and adjust your emergency fund as your financial situation changes.

Chapter 4: Paying Off Debt

Debt can be a significant burden, affecting not only one's financial well-being but also mental health and overall quality of life. However, with a little discipline and planning, it is possible to pay off debt and achieve financial freedom. In this article, we will explore different strategies for paying off debt, including the snowball method and the avalanche method.

The Burden of Debt: Breaking Free with Discipline and Planning

Understanding Debt

★ Before we dive into debt repayment strategies, it's essential to understand the nature of debt. Debt is essentially borrowing money from an individual or institution to finance a purchase or expense, with the promise to repay the amount borrowed, along with interest and fees. There are two main types of debt: good debt and bad debt.

- Good debt refers to debt used to purchase assets that appreciate in value over time, such as a home or education. Good debt can be beneficial as it can increase one's net worth.
- Bad debt, on the other hand, refers to debt used to finance non-essential purchases or expenses, such as credit card debt or personal loans. Bad debt can lead to financial trouble and stress.

Debt Repayment Strategies

There are several debt repayment strategies that individuals can use to pay off their debts. Two popular methods are the snowball method and the avalanche method.

The Snowball Method

The snowball method was popularized by financial expert Dave Ramsey. This method involves paying off debts in a specific order, starting with the smallest balance first. Here's how it works:

1. List all debts, including the balance and interest rate for each.

2. Sort the debts by balance, from smallest to largest.

3. Pay the minimum payment on all debts except the smallest one.

4. Apply as much money as possible towards the smallest debt until it is paid off.

5. Once the smallest debt is paid off, move on to the next smallest debt and repeat the process.

The snowball method provides a psychological boost as individuals can quickly see progress and achieve small victories along the way. It also helps build momentum and motivation to continue paying off debts.

The Avalanche Method

The avalanche method involves paying off debts in a specific order, starting with the one with the highest interest rate. Here's how it works:

1. List all debts, including the balance and interest rate for each.
2. Sort the debts by interest rate, from highest to lowest.
3. Pay the minimum payment on all debts except the one with the highest interest rate.
4. Apply as much money as possible towards the debt with the highest interest rate until it is paid off.
5. Once the highest-interest debt is paid off, move on to the next highest-interest debt and repeat the process.

The avalanche method can save individuals more money in interest payments over time compared to the snowball method. However, it may not provide the same psychological boost as seeing progress on smaller debts first.

Additional Strategies

In addition to the snowball and avalanche methods, there are several other strategies that individuals can use to pay off their debts:

- **Debt consolidation:** Combining multiple debts into a single loan with a lower interest rate or a single monthly payment can simplify finances and reduce stress.
- **Debt negotiation:** Negotiating with creditors to reduce interest rates or fees can save individuals money on their debts.
- **Increase income:** Increasing income through a side hustle or salary increase can provide more money available for debt repayment.

- ***Decrease expenses:*** Reducing expenses by cutting back on non-essential spending can free up more money for debt repayment.

Tips for Paying Off Debt

Paying off debt requires discipline and commitment. Here are some tips to help individuals stay on track:

- Create a budget: Track income and expenses to ensure that there is enough money available for debt repayment.
- Prioritize needs over wants: Focus on paying off essential expenses before discretionary spending.
- Automate payments: Set up automatic payments to ensure consistent payments are made on time.
- Build an emergency fund: Save three-to-six months' worth of living expenses in an easily accessible savings account to avoid going further into debt when unexpected expenses arise.

Paying off debt requires discipline and planning, but it is possible with the right strategies and mindset. The snowball and avalanche methods are two popular approaches that individuals can use to pay off their debts. By prioritizing needs over wants, creating a budget, automating payments, and building an emergency fund, individuals can stay on track and achieve financial freedom. Remember that paying off debt is a journey that takes time, patience, and perseverance, but the benefits of financial freedom make it well worth the effort.

Chapter 5: Saving for the Future

Saving for the future is a crucial aspect of personal finance, as it enables individuals to achieve their long-term goals, such as retirement, buying a house, or funding their children's education. In this chapter, we will explore the importance of saving for the future and provide practical tips on how to do so effectively.

Why Save for the Future?

- Saving for the future is essential because it allows individuals to:

1. Achieve financial independence: By saving for the future, individuals can reduce their reliance on others and have more control over their financial decisions.

2. Plan for unexpected expenses: Life is unpredictable, and unexpected expenses can arise at any time. Having a savings buffer can help individuals weather financial storms.

3. Retire comfortably: Saving for retirement ensures that individuals have enough resources to maintain their standard of living in their golden years.

4. Fund important milestones: Whether it's a down payment on a house, your child's education, or a dream vacation, saving for specific goals can help make them a reality.

Step 1: Setting Savings Goals

- To start saving for the future, it's essential to set specific, measurable, achievable, relevant, and time-bound (SMART) goals. Consider the following questions when setting your savings goals:

1. What do you want to save for?

2. How much do you need to save?

3. When do you need to save it by?

4. What are the potential consequences of not achieving your goal?

Examples of SMART savings goals include:

* Save $10,000 for a down payment on a house in 2 years

* Save $5,000 for a dream vacation in 3 years

* Save $1 million for retirement by age 65

Step 2: Automating Your Savings

Automating your savings is an effective way to ensure that you stick to your goals. Consider the following strategies:

1. Set up automatic transfers: Set up automatic transfers from your checking account to your savings or investment accounts.
2. Use payroll deductions: If you're employed, consider setting up payroll deductions for your savings contributions.
3. Take advantage of employer matching: If your employer offers a 401(k) or other retirement plan matching program, contribute enough to maximize the match.
4. Use mobile banking apps: Utilize mobile banking apps that allow you to set reminders and automate savings transfers.

Additional Tips for Effective Savings

1. Prioritize needs over wants: Be honest with yourself about what you need versus what you want. Prioritize saving for essential goals over discretionary spending.
2. Avoid lifestyle inflation: As your income increases, avoid the temptation to inflate your lifestyle by spending more on luxuries. Instead, direct excess funds towards your savings goals.
3. Consider tax-advantaged accounts: Utilize tax-advantaged accounts such as 401(k), IRA, or Roth IRA for retirement savings and other long-term goals.

4. Diversify your investments: Spread your investments across different asset classes to minimize risk and maximize returns.
5. Monitor and adjust: Regularly review your progress towards your goals and adjust your strategy as needed.

Common Obstacles to Saving

1. Lack of discipline: Saving requires discipline and self-control. Avoid impulse purchases and stay focused on your goals.
2. Financial stress: High levels of financial stress can lead to decreased motivation to save. Practice stress-reducing techniques such as meditation or deep breathing.
3. Uncertainty about investment options: Feeling overwhelmed by investment options can lead to inaction. Consider consulting with a financial advisor or using online resources to educate yourself.
4. Fear of missing out (FOMO): Fear of missing out on potential investments or opportunities can lead to impulsive decisions. Stay informed but avoid emotional decisions.

Saving for the future is essential for achieving financial security and independence. By setting SMART goals, automating your savings, and avoiding common obstacles, you can make progress towards achieving your financial objectives. Remember to prioritize needs over wants, avoid lifestyle inflation, and diversify your investments to maximize returns.

By following these steps and staying committed to your goals, you can build a secure financial foundation that will serve you well throughout your life.

Additional Resources

- **Online resources:**
    - The Balance: A comprehensive personal finance website with articles on saving and investing

    - NerdWallet: A personal finance website with calculators and tools for saving and investing

- Investopedia: A financial education website with articles on investing and personal finance
- **Books:**
  - "The Automatic Millionaire" by David Bach: A practical guide to automating your finances
  - "A Random Walk Down Wall Street" by Burton G. Malkiel: A comprehensive guide to investing
  - "Your Money or Your Life" by Vicki Robin and Joe Dominguez: A comprehensive approach to achieving financial independence

Chapter 6: Investing in Your Future

Investing is a crucial aspect of building wealth over time. It involves putting your money into assets that have a good chance of increasing in value over time, providing a return on your investment. In this chapter, we will explore different investment options, including stocks, bonds, and mutual funds, and provide tips on how to get started.

What is Investing?

Investing is putting your money into assets that can grow in value over time. This can include stocks, bonds, real estate, commodities, and other financial instruments. The goal of investing is to generate a return on your investment, which can help you achieve your financial goals.

Types of Investments

There are many types of investments available, each with its own set of benefits and risks. Here are some of the most common types of investments:

1. **Stocks**: Stocks represent ownership of a company and give you a claim on a portion of its assets and profits. They can be traded on stock exchanges and offer the potential for long-term growth.

2. **Bonds**: Bonds are debt securities issued by companies or governments to raise capital. They offer a fixed rate of return in the form of interest payments and the return of principal at maturity.

3. **Mutual Funds**: Mutual funds are investment vehicles that pool money from many investors to invest in a diversified portfolio of stocks, bonds, or other securities.

4. **Real Estate**: Real estate investments involve buying and holding physical property, such as rental properties or vacation homes.

5. **Commodities**: Commodities are physical goods, such as gold, oil, or agricultural products.

6. **Index Funds**: Index funds track a specific market index, such as the S&P 500, to provide broad diversification and reduce risk.

7. **Exchange-Traded Funds (ETFs)**: ETFs are traded on stock exchanges like stocks and offer diversification and flexibility.

☺ ***Getting Started with Investing***

If you're new to investing, it's essential to start with a solid understanding of your financial goals and risk tolerance. Here are some steps to get started:

1. **Set Financial Goals:** Define your financial goals, such as saving for retirement or a down payment on a house.

2. **Assess Your Risk Tolerance:** Determine how much risk you're willing to take on by considering your age, income, and financial situation.

3. **Choose an Investment Account:** Open an investment account with a reputable brokerage firm or online trading platform.

4. **Select Your Investments:** Choose investments that align with your goals and risk tolerance, such as index funds or individual stocks.

5. **Start Small:** Begin with a small investment amount and gradually increase it over time.

6. **Monitor and Adjust:** Regularly monitor your investments and adjust your portfolio as needed to ensure it remains aligned with your goals.

Tips for Investing Success

Here are some additional tips to help you succeed in investing:

1. **Diversify Your Portfolio:** Spread your investments across different asset classes to minimize risk.
2. **Research and Understand:** Take the time to research and understand the investments you're considering.
3. **Don't Put All Your Eggs in One Basket:** Avoid putting all your investments into one type of security or sector.
4. **Be Patient:** Investing is a long-term game; avoid making impulsive decisions based on short-term market fluctuations.
5. **Rebalance Your Portfolio:** Regularly rebalance your portfolio to ensure it remains aligned with your goals and risk tolerance.
6. **Keep Costs Low:** Minimize fees and expenses by choosing low-cost index funds or ETFs.

Investing is a powerful tool for building wealth over time. By understanding different types of investments and getting started with a solid plan, you can achieve your financial goals. Remember to diversify your portfolio, research and understand your investments, be patient, rebalance your portfolio regularly, and keep costs low.

Additional Resources

- "A Random Walk Down Wall Street" by Burton G. Malkiel
- "The Little Book of Common-Sense Investing" by John C. Bogle
- "The Intelligent Investor" by Benjamin Graham
- "Investopedia" website

Quiz Time!

Test your knowledge by taking this quiz:

1. What is the primary goal of investing?

a) To make quick profits

b) To build wealth over time

c) To avoid risk

d) To diversify my portfolio

Answer: **b) To build wealth over time**

2. Which type of investment offers a fixed rate of return in the form of interest payments?

a) Stock

b) Bond

c) Mutual Fund

d) ETF

Answer: b) Bond

3. What is the best way to get started with investing?

a) By opening an investment account with a reputable brokerage firm

b) By selecting individual stocks

c) By investing all my money at once

d) By avoiding investing altogether

Answer: **a) By opening an investment account with a reputable brokerage firm**

Chapter 7: Protecting your Money!

Protecting your money is essential, whether it's from theft, fraud, or unforeseen circumstances. This chapter will provide tips on how to safeguard your finances, including using strong passwords, monitoring your accounts, and purchasing insurance.

As we have discussed throughout this book, having a solid financial foundation is crucial for achieving your financial goals. However, protecting your money is just as important. Unfortunately, financial crimes and unforeseen circumstances can happen to anyone, leaving you with significant financial losses. In this chapter, we'll provide you with practical tips on how to safeguard your finances, including using strong passwords, monitoring your accounts, and purchasing insurance.

Strong Passwords

Using strong passwords is the first line of defense against financial fraud. Here are some tips to help you create and use strong passwords:

1. Length matters: Aim for passwords that are at least 12 characters long. The longer the password, the harder it is to crack.

2. Mix it up: Combine uppercase and lowercase letters, numbers, and special characters to create a complex password.

3. Avoid common words: Don't use easily guessed words like your name, birthdate, or common passwords like "qwerty" or "123456."

4. Use a password manager: Consider using a password manager like LastPass or 1Password to generate and store unique, complex passwords for each account.

5. Change them regularly: Update your passwords every 60-90 days (about 3 months) to minimize the risk of unauthorized access.

Monitoring Your Accounts

Regularly monitoring your accounts is essential to detect and prevent financial fraud. Here are some steps you can take:

1. Check your statements: Review your bank and credit card statements regularly to ensure all transactions are legitimate.

2. Set up alerts: Many banks and credit card companies offer alert services that notify you of unusual activity or suspicious transactions.

3. Use account aggregation tools: Services like Mint or Personal Capital allow you to track all your accounts in one place.

4. Monitor credit reports: Check your credit report annually to ensure its accurate and free of errors.

Purchasing Insurance

Insurance can provide financial protection against unforeseen circumstances like accidents, illnesses, or job loss. Here are some types of insurance to consider:

1. Health insurance: If you're employed, consider purchasing a health insurance plan through your employer or the Affordable Care Act marketplace.

2. Disability insurance: If you're self-employed or have a variable income, disability insurance can provide financial protection if you're unable to work.

3. Life insurance: Term life insurance can provide financial security for your loved ones in the event of your passing.

4. Home and auto insurance: Make sure you have adequate coverage for your home and vehicles.

Additional Tips

In addition to using strong passwords, monitoring your accounts, and purchasing insurance, here are some additional tips to protect your money:

1. Use two-factor authentication: Two-factor authentication adds an extra layer of security by requiring a second form of verification (e.g., a code sent to your phone) in addition to your password.

2. Keep software up-to-date: Ensure your operating system, browser, and antivirus software are updated with the latest security patches.

3. Be cautious with public Wi-Fi: Avoid conducting sensitive financial transactions over public Wi-Fi networks.

4. Shred documents: Shred any documents containing personal or financial information before disposing of them.

5. Freeze credit reports: Consider freezing your credit reports with the three major credit reporting agencies (Equifax, Experian, and TransUnion) to prevent identity theft.

Protecting your money is a vital part of achieving financial stability and security. By following these tips on using strong passwords, monitoring your accounts, and purchasing insurance, you can significantly reduce the risk of financial fraud and unforeseen circumstances. Remember to always be vigilant and take proactive steps to protect your financial well-being.

Additional Resources

- Federal Trade Commission (FTC): www.ftc.gov

- Identity Theft Resource Center: www.idtheftcenter.org

- National Foundation for Credit Counseling: www.nfcc.org

Action Plan

1. Review your current password practices and update them according to the tips provided in this chapter.

2. Set up account alerts with your bank and credit card company to notify you of unusual activity.

3. Check your credit report annually to ensure its accurate and free of errors. Consider purchasing insurance policies that align with your financial goals and risk tolerance.

5. Take additional steps to protect yourself from financial fraud by using two-factor authentication, keeping software up-to-date, and being cautious with public Wi-Fi.

By following these steps and tips, you'll be well on your way to protecting your money and achieving long-term financial stability.

Thank you for taking the time to read Mastering Your Money. I hope that the tips and insights provided in this book will help you on your journey to financial literacy and freedom. Remember, financial literacy is a lifelong journey, and there is always more to learn. Keep exploring, keep learning, and keep striving for financial success.

Additional Resources:

To further your financial literacy journey, here are some additional resources:

* Investopedia: A comprehensive financial education website that offers articles, videos, and courses on a wide range of financial topics.

* The Total Money Makeover by Dave Ramsey: A best-selling book that provides a practical plan for getting out of debt and building wealth.

* The Simple Path to Wealth by JL Collins: A straightforward guide to investing and building wealth.

* The Millionaire Next Door by Thomas J. Stanley and William D. Danko: A classic book that explores the habits and traits of successful millionaires.

* Your local library: Many libraries offer financial literacy resources, including books, e-books, and online courses.

Appendix:

Here are some additional tips and insights that didn't make it into the main chapters but are still worth mentioning:

* Automate your savings: Set up automatic transfers from your checking account to your savings account to make saving easier and more consistent.

* Use cash instead of credit: Using cash instead of credit can help you stick to your budget and avoid overspending.

* Negotiate your bills: Many bills, such as cable and internet, are negotiable. Do not be afraid to call your service providers and ask for a better deal.

* Avoid lifestyle inflation: As your income increases, it can be tempting to upgrade your lifestyle. However, avoiding lifestyle inflation and continuing to live below your means can help you build wealth faster.

* Educate yourself: Financial literacy is a continually evolving field, and there's always more to learn. Stay up-to-date with the latest financial news and trends by reading books, articles, and blogs.

Thank you for reading Mastering Your Money. I hope this book has provided you with the tools and knowledge you need to manage your money effectively and live a financially fulfilled life. Remember, financial literacy is a lifelong journey, and every step you take towards mastering your money is a step towards a brighter future.

www.ingramcontent.com/pod-product-compliance
Lightning Source LLC
Chambersburg PA
CBHW082242220526
45479CB00005B/1313